M000204106

The Risks of SOCIAL MEDIA

SOCIAL MEDIA *Deception*

Bradley Steffens

ReferencePoint
Press®

San Diego, CA

ReferencePoint Press®

About the Author

Bradley Steffens is a novelist, a poet, and an award-winning author of more than sixty nonfiction books for children and young adults.

For more information, contact:
ReferencePoint Press, Inc.
PO Box 27779
San Diego, CA 92198
www.ReferencePointPress.com

Picture Credits:

Cover: Shutterstock.com
 5: mk1one/Shutterstock.com
 9: zstock/Shutterstock.com
13: fizkes/Shutterstock.com
17: z katz/Shutterstock.com
21: Neil Bussey/Shutterstock.com
24: rawf8/Shutterstock.com
26: Jarretera/Shutterstock.com
32: Shutterstock.com
34: s_bukley/Shutterstock.com
39: A3pfamily/Shutterstock.com
45: Maury Aaseng
49: dennizn/Shutterstock.com
51: Aaron-Schwartz/Shutterstock.com

LIBRARY OF CONGRESS CATALOGING-IN-PUBLICATION DATA

Names: Steffens, Bradley - author.
Title: Social media deception / by Bradley Steffens.
Description: San Diego, CA : ReferencePoint Press, [2021] | Series: The risks of social media | Includes bibliographical references and index.
Identifiers: LCCN 2020021687| | ISBN 9781682828533 (library binding) | ISBN 9781682828540 (ebook)
Subjects: LCSH: Social media--Juvenile literature. | Online deception --Juvenile literature.

Contents

A Crisis of Truth

In June 2017 anonymous posters on the online forum 4chan falsely reported that Vitalik Buterin, founder and chief executive officer of cryptocurrency company Ethereum, had died in a car crash. The fake news story spread through social media like wildfire. Fearing a collapse of Ethereum's digital currency, people who owned it began selling it at lower and lower prices to get whatever they could out of their investment. Within hours, the currency, known as ETH, lost $4 billion of its value. This allowed speculators—including the people behind the fake news story—to purchase ETH at bargain prices. When Buterin quashed the rumors of his death, ETH bounced back, immediately regaining 50 percent of its lost value and eventually returning to its former highs. Those who had purchased ETH at its low point during the hoax made a huge profit as the value of their digital tokens rose dramatically.

Sowing Doubts and Confusion

The Buterin death hoax is an example of social media deception. It reveals how people with bad intentions can use social media's instant communications to fool segments of the public for personal gain. The motive is not always money. Political parties and their allies use fake news to influence voters before elections. Enemies of businesses use social media to defame corporations to cripple their sales and reduce their profits. Proponents of alternative medicine make unproven claims as a way of undermining confidence in traditional medicine.

The purpose of social media deception is often to sow confusion. "It's important to note that the goal of these tools is not necessarily to create consistent and believable alternative facts, but to create plausible levels of doubt in actual facts," says Jamais Cascio, distinguished fellow at the Institute for the Future. "The crisis we face about 'truth' and reliable facts is predicated less on the ability to get people to believe the *wrong* thing as it is on the ability to get people to *doubt* the right thing."[1]

A Lack of Trust

The prevalence of false and deceptive information is creating a crisis in the United States. People are having a hard time knowing what and whom to believe. Political leaders have gone beyond interpreting facts for their own benefit to inventing them out of thin air. The government has been caught suppressing truthful information that contradicts official statements. Even scientists have been caught falsifying or exaggerating data to support their pet

Anonymous posters falsely reported the death of the chief executive officer of cryptocurrency company Ethereum. Ethereum stock crashed at the news, allowing the posters an opportunity to purchase shares at bargain prices.

theories and beliefs. Social media makes the situation worse by spreading false words, pictures, and videos so quickly that opinions are formed before the whole truth is known.

Not all social media deception is aimed at affecting public opinion. Some is designed to fool individuals, usually as a way of stealing their money. Many online scams entice the social media user into giving up personal information in order to benefit in some way. Sometimes the promised benefits are minor: learning the results of an online quiz, receiving a coffee shop gift card, or even seeing an unusual photograph. Other times, the enticements are larger: a fortune in lottery winnings or the chance to date someone with movie-star good looks. These scams prey on people's basic wants and needs—their basic curiosity, their desire for easy money, their longing for love and happiness.

Experts are divided on what can be done about social media deception. Some are optimistic that software programs can be devised that will identify and eliminate fake news and other forms of false information circulating on the internet. Others are doubtful. Part of the problem is technical. Purveyors of deception can always adapt to whatever measures are used against them. "Many excellent methods will be developed to improve the information environment, but the history of online systems shows that bad actors can and will always find ways around them,"[2] says Paul N. Edwards, Perry Fellow in International Security at Stanford University.

Another part of the problem is that people are not ready to wage all-out war on disinformation. "There is no market for the truth," says an executive consultant based in North America. "The public isn't motivated to seek out verified, vetted information. They are happy hearing what confirms their views."[3] Until people care about getting the truth, social media deception will persist.

> "Many excellent methods will be developed to improve the information environment, but the history of online systems shows that bad actors can and will always find ways around them."[2]
>
> —Paul N. Edwards, Perry Fellow in International Security at Stanford University

Chapter One

Deception and Distrust

On March 29, 2020, a retired Los Angeles firefighter posted an article about the 2019 novel coronavirus on Facebook for his friends and family to see. "This is from a immunologist at Johns Hopkins University," the post begins. "Maybe he knows more than some. Just wow."[4] The article begins: "Feeling confused as to why Coronavirus is a bigger deal than Seasonal flu? Here it is in a nutshell. I hope this helps. Feel free to share this to others who don't understand."[5] What follows is a discussion of the coronavirus, which causes the disease known as COVID-19. By this time, the virus and disease had spread through Wuhan, China, where it was first identified; was taking lives in Europe; and was sweeping through the United States.

The article states that the coronavirus was mutating at a faster rate than other viruses and that this is what made it more dangerous than the common influenza virus. "One day, at an animal market, in Wuhan China, in December 2019, it mutated and made the jump from animal to people," states the article. "At first, only animals could give it to a person. . . . But here is the scary part . . . in just TWO WEEKS it mutated again and gained the ability to jump from human to human. Scientists call this quick ability, 'slippery.'"[6]

With its blend of scientific language and nontechnical terms like "bigger deal," "nutshell," and "slippery," the article appealed to people who wanted to understand the coronavirus but were confused by explanations in the traditional news media. The article went "viral," spreading from person to person through social media like the virus it was discussing.

False Information

There is a problem with the coronavirus article, however: much of what it says is not true. The coronavirus did not need to mutate to make the jump from animals to the human population. The animal version of the virus already had the ability to recognize and stick to a protein called ACE2, which is found on the surface of human cells, giving the virus a pathway to infection. "It had already found its best way of being a [human] virus,"[7] says Matthew Friedman of the University of Maryland School of Medicine.

The virus was not mutating as rapidly as the article suggests, either. "The virus has been remarkably stable given how much transmission we've seen," says Lisa Gralinski, a professor of epidemiology at the University of North Carolina. Gralinski explains that the virus is stable because it is effective in its current state. "There's no evolutionary pressure on the virus to transmit better," she explains. "It's doing a great job of spreading around the world right now."[8]

The article makes the dire prediction that the fast-mutating nature of the virus would make it especially difficult to stop with a vaccine. This is also false, according to Matt Koci, a professor of immunology, virology, and host-pathogen interactions at North Carolina State University. Koci points out that even if the virus mutates, vaccine makers will adapt to the change. "We do this for [the] flu, so we should be able to do it for this [novel coronavirus] too," Koci says. "We have a pretty good idea of how we need to change the vaccine each year to keep pace. It may take a while until we understand the differences in coronavirus strains at the same level, but we'll get there."[9]

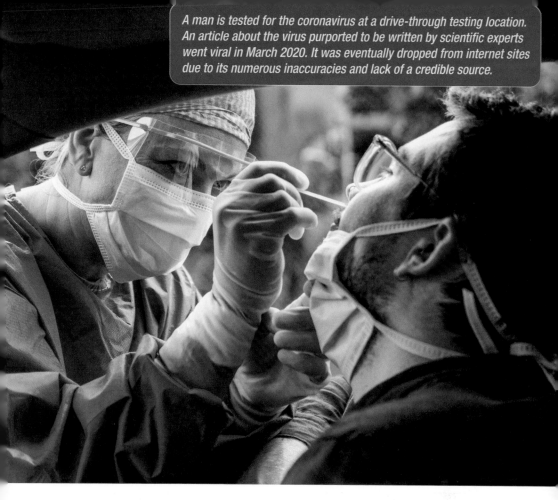

A man is tested for the coronavirus at a drive-through testing location. An article about the virus purported to be written by scientific experts went viral in March 2020. It was eventually dropped from internet sites due to its numerous inaccuracies and lack of a credible source.

Going Viral

Despite its numerous errors, the coronavirus article was posted on the question-and-answer website Quora; showed up on dozens of blogs, bulletin boards, and websites; and was even quoted in a news story published by the *Livingston Parish News*, a newspaper in Denham Springs, Louisiana. Later, however, the newspaper deleted the quote, stating, "The original statement . . . could not be cited appropriately and has been removed from this story."[10]

The article's folksy charm was one reason for its viral success. The author uses plain language and even slang, including "gonna" in place of "going to." Another reason for the article's popularity is the claim that it came from an immunologist at Johns Hopkins

In April 2020 Facebook announced a crackdown on false stories regarding the COVID-19 pandemic. The company removed links to a false story on the News NT website that claimed 21 million people had died from COVID-19 in China—a number forty-five hundred times greater than the official count. The original links garnered only 520 interactions and 100 shares on Facebook, but that was not the end of the story. The Technology and Social Change Research Project at the Harvard University Kennedy School of Government's Shorenstein Center found the fake news item living on in the form of "zombie content." The News NT page was automatically saved to the Wayback Machine, a digital archive of the World Wide Web operated by the nonprofit Internet Archive. The page cannot be found through normal web searches, but a link to it can be shared. As of April 30, 2020, the link had received 649,000 interactions and 118,000 shares on Facebook. "There are several explanations for this hidden virality," writes Joan Donovan, director of the Shorenstein Center. "Some people use the Internet Archive to evade blocking of banned domains in their home country, but it is not simply about censorship. Others are seeking to get around fact-checking and algorithmic demotion of content."

Joan Donovan, "Covid Hoaxes Are Using a Loophole to Stay Alive—Even After Content Is Deleted," *MIT Technology Review*, April 30, 2020. www.technologyreview.com.

University. The attribution gave the article credibility, since Johns Hopkins University is home to one of the nation's leading medical schools. But a third reason the article spread quickly is a lack of critical thinking by the people who shared it. The article contains many hints that it is more "fake" than "news," but readers ignored the warning signs.

Anatomy of Deceit

The first clue that the article is not credible, as the the *Livingston Parish News* notes, is the lack of a verifiable source. The author's name is not provided. This is a common feature of fake news stories, and it should be a huge red flag to the reader. An authoritative article on a scientific topic would be attributed to the scientist or team of scientists who wrote it. The coronavirus article actually is attributed to at least three different authorities in various social media posts: the Johns Hopkins immunologist, a respiratory therapist from Nashville, Tennessee, and a person who one social media poster says "has now retired from a career in a top position at Vanderbilt Hospital in Nashville, TN."[11] On some websites, the article appears without any attribution but with a disclaimer, such as, "Copied and pasted from elsewhere"[12] or "I saw a great post about it on FB, I'll post it here."[13] The lack of a consistent source is a clear sign that the article is not what it purports to be.

The spelling, punctuation, and typography of the coronavirus article also suggest that the information it contains might not be credible. An article written by an active or even retired university scientist during a time of crisis would most likely be issued by the school's press office and would be carefully proofread. At the very least, the article would be checked for errors by a secretary or perhaps a postdoctoral researcher. While such an article might contain a typographic error or two, it would rarely contain dozens of errors, as the coronavirus piece does. For example, the very first line of the viral post refers to "a immunologist" instead of "an immunologist." Misspellings appear throughout the piece: "thats" instead of "that's," "it's" instead of "its," and so on. Capitalization is not regular, either. The word "human" is incorrectly capitalized in the middle of a sentence. The first words of many sentences are not capitalized as required. And capital letters are used for emphasis in an unprofessional way: "in just TWO WEEKS it mutated again."[14]

The coronavirus piece also has far too many grammatical errors to have come from a reputable source. Many complete sentences are separated by ellipses instead of periods. Although this could be done once or twice for effect, it occurs twelve times in the article: "Now, here comes this Coronavirus . . . it existed in animals only" and "it can now transfer human to human . . . once that happens . . . we have a new contagion phase." Sometimes commas are used to join two complete sentences in what is known as a comma splice. At other times single commas separate the subject and verb of a sentence, contrary to the rules of grammar: "Novel viruses, come from animals," and "this particular mutated animal virus, changed itself."[15] These and other grammatical errors should have served as a warning to social media users that the article was not from a scientific authority.

Fearmongering

The biggest clue that the viral post is fake is the use of slang that scientists would not be likely to employ. An immunologist is unlikely to call a virus "slippery." At another point, the author refers to the virus as "a lung eater."[16] While the coronavirus does damage lung cells, the term "lung eater" is sensationalistic. Sensationalism is the hallmark of fake news.

Contrary to what the post's introduction promises—a reasoned discussion of the pandemic—the writing seems designed to stir up fear. Near the end, it states that "the human immune system doesn't recognize it [the virus] so, we can't fight it off." This statement is not true. By suggesting that the virus is unstoppable, the author is inciting unwarranted fear—a technique known as fearmongering. At another point, the author writes that "if it mutates again (and it will). Who is to say, what it will do next."[17] The implication is that human beings are helpless before the ever-changing virus—another example of fearmongering.

It is not clear what motivated the author to write and distribute the article. It ends with the same commonsense suggestion that the federal, state, and local governments were making: to stay at home to decrease the spread of the virus. This suggests that the article was not written to sow doubt about the government or the medical establishment, as many fake news stories are. The post did not refer to any product or home remedy, so it did not seem to be designed to make money, either. The most logical conclusion is that its creator launched it simply to see how far in the social networks it would go. Some people practicing social media deception do it for the thrill of seeing if they can create something that goes viral. The article's closing suggests that this was the case. It asks readers to pass it along. "Stay home folks," it reads, "and share this to those that just are not catching on."[18]

Appealing to Ego

The article's closing plea is also a staple of fake news. It appeals to the reader's ego. It suggests that those who have read the article are smarter than, and therefore superior to, those who have not read it. It appeals to the readers' desire to be looked up to by their peers, which they believe they can achieve by sharing the secret, inside information. "Human beings are not wired to be logical creatures that pursue objective truth," says Jonathan Rauch, a senior fellow at the Brookings Institution, an American research group. "We're wired to be tribal creatures that try and ingratiate ourselves with our group and improve our status within that group."[19]

> "Human beings are not wired to be logical creatures that pursue objective truth. We're wired to be tribal creatures that try and ingratiate ourselves with our group and improve our status within that group."[19]
>
> —Jonathan Rauch, senior fellow at the Brookings Institution

On April 21, 2020, the Senate Select Committee on Intelligence chair released the fourth volume in the committee's bipartisan investigation into Russian interference in American elections. The report warns that Russia will continue to post fake news on social media and elsewhere to influence US elections and that this activity should be considered "the new normal." The report states:

> While the Committee notes that "new normal" is an imprecise term, the Committee found that this section convincingly argues that Russia's use of active measures to target elections has been widely applied outside the United States over the past decade. The analytic line on "new normal" serves as both prediction and warning, and the Committee notes that IC [Intelligence Committee] and open source reporting has revealed much evidence to reinforce the IC's 2016 assessments. The final analytic line of the ICA [Intelligence Community Assessment] states: "We assess Moscow will apply lessons learned from its campaign aimed at the U.S. presidential election to future influence efforts in the U.S. and worldwide. We assess the Russian intelligence services would have seen their election influence as at least a qualified success because of their perceived ability to impact public discussion in the U.S."

Senate Select Committee on Intelligence, *Report of the Select Committee on Intelligence, United States Senate, on Russian Active Measures Campaigns and Interference in the 2016 U.S. Election.* Vol. 4, *Review of the Intelligence Community Assessment, with Additional Views.* Washington, DC: Senate Select Committee on Intelligence, 2020, pp. 118–19. www.intelligence.senate.gov.

Reader attitudes play a major role in the proliferation of fake news reports like the coronavirus story. Many people prefer quick, easy reads to more detailed reports. They often lack or fail to use critical-thinking skills, such as the ability to recognize scare tactics. "Most users just read the headline, comment and share without digesting the entire article or thinking critically about its content (if they read it at all),"[20] states a project leader for a science institute who responded to a Pew Research Center survey on fake news. The lack of critical thinking enables false stories to spread quickly through social media.

While the coronavirus story was posted on websites across the internet, it gained most of its readers through social media. False and deceptive stories have greater impact than ever before, in part because more people are relying on social media for their news than ever before. An October 2019 survey by the Pew Research Center found that 55 percent of US adults often or sometimes get their news from social media, up from 47 percent in 2018. The 2019 survey was the first time that a majority of adults surveyed by Pew said social media played a significant role in their news habits. Facebook is the dominant social media news source, Pew reports. About half (52 percent) of all US adults get at least some of their news on Facebook.

Information Silos

Another factor in the spread of disinformation is that more and more people trust fewer and fewer news sources. The Pew Research Center analyzed 376 million Facebook users' interactions with over nine hundred news outlets. The researchers found that people tend to seek information that aligns with their views. This means that people are spending their time in information silos, isolated from opinions that are different from theirs. They only hear opinions that agree with their own, a phenomenon known as living in an echo chamber. "People on systems like Facebook are increasingly forming into 'echo chambers' of those who think alike," says Starr Roxanne Hiltz, a retired distinguished professor of information systems at the New Jersey Institute of Technology. "They will keep unfriending those who don't, and passing on rumors and fake news that agrees with their point of view."[21] By living in information silos and listening to echo chambers, social media users are at risk of believing false information that is targeted at them.

"People on systems like Facebook are increasingly forming into 'echo chambers' of those who think alike. They will keep unfriending those who don't, and passing on rumors and fake news that agrees with their point of view."[21]

—Starr Roxanne Hiltz, retired professor of information systems at the New Jersey Institute of Technology

Social media companies allow advertisers—including political parties and activists—to target their ads by geographic area, age, gender, and the interest groups that users belong to and the types of things they "like." Using this information, fake news posters can aim false messages at the people who are most likely to read them and believe them. For example, a fake news report about cutting Social Security benefits can be targeted at seniors who depend on such funds to pay their bills. A fake news story about the dangers of vaccines can be targeted at new parents who might be deciding about vaccinating their newborns. These messages reach people in the silos they have built for themselves. When a social media user shares a story, it reaches even more like-minded people in the same information silo. Because the story was shared by a friend, it will be read with less skepticism and less critical thinking than a regular news story might.

The separation into silos also causes people not only to accept information that is false but also to reject information that is true because it conflicts with their preconceived ideas and beliefs. Those practicing social media deception like this trait because it makes it easier to circulate fake news stories within the silos. Some social media deceivers use false or exaggerated information to deepen and harden these silos, preventing the give-and-take of meaningful discussion and keeping people entrenched in their separate camps. This makes them easier to manipulate with propaganda and fake news.

Creating Chaos

Some of the bad actors in social media disinformation campaigns include politicians, political parties, social activists, and nation-states that want to disrupt elections and confuse the public about political, social, and economic issues. For example, in 2018 Facebook staff members told the Senate and House intelligence committees that a Russian group called the Internet Research Agency purchased at least three thousand ads in the run-up to the 2016 presidential election. Some of the ads attacked

Democratic candidate Hillary Clinton, some attacked Republican candidate Donald Trump, and others spread inflammatory messages on sensitive subjects such as immigration and race. The ads targeted Facebook users from specific backgrounds in key presidential battleground states such as Pennsylvania, Wisconsin, and Virginia.

Ads placed in Texas show how messages can be targeted to social media users who share specific beliefs. For example, Facebook revealed that a Russian-linked page called "Heart of Texas," which supports the secession of Texas from the United States, sponsored ads that portrayed Hillary Clinton as an obstacle to Texas independence. "Get ready to secede!" read the headline of one ad. It continued: "Fellow Texans! It's time to say a strong NO to the establishment robbers. . . . The establishment thinks they can treat us like stupid sheep but they are wrong. We won't put up with

Facebook staff members told US intelligence agencies that one Russian group purchased at least three thousand ads in the run-up to the 2016 presidential election. Many of the ads attacked Democratic candidate Hillary Clinton (pictured).

this anymore."[22] Representative Joaquin Castro, a Democrat from Texas, denounced the Russian interference in the election:

> These Facebook advertisements released today are the most brazen example of Russia's intent to weaponize our social media platforms, divide and polarize our political system, and exploit frustration and anger held by the American public. The advertisements also demonstrate the IRA's (Russia's Internet Research Agency) multifaceted approach that capitalized on racial, ethnic, political and state cleavages, as evidenced in the creation of specific pages dedicated to the Texas secessionist movement.[23]

In April 2020 a bipartisan report from the Senate Select Committee on Intelligence warned that Russian interference was likely to occur again in the 2020 elections. "Russia's aggressive interference efforts should be considered 'the new normal,'"[24] stated the report. Richard Burr, a North Carolina Republican who was chair of the committee, called for the US intelligence agencies, Congress, and social media providers to remain alert to Russian efforts to use social media to influence voters. "With the 2020 presidential election approaching, it's more important than ever that we remain vigilant against the threat of interference from hostile foreign actors,"[25] said Burr.

Vigilance is not easy, and this is a major reason why fake news articles spread through social media. Many people log on to social media to relax. If they can pick up a tidbit of information that makes them feel good, so much the better. Critical thinking requires effort and discipline—more effort than most people are willing to expend for something as seemingly nonthreatening as social media. With their defenses down, social media users are vulnerable to those who make online deception their full-time job.

Chapter Two

Falling for Scams

Caroline Fanning wanted to go to a blacklight rave being held in a Brooklyn, New York, warehouse in the summer of 2018. All her friends were going, and at the last minute she was able to get someone to cover her shift at work, so she could go, too. There was a problem, though. The event was sold out, and Fanning did not have a ticket. Fortunately, she knew where to look for one. She went to the rave's "Event" page on Facebook and began scrolling through the posts.

Overcoming Skepticism

Dozens of people were trying to sell tickets to the Brooklyn rave, but they all were charging several times the original price of the twenty-five-dollar tickets. All except for one poster. He wrote that something had come up and he was no longer able to use his ticket. He was willing to trade it for a thirty-dollar Amazon gift card. Fanning bought the gift card, but she was wary about handing it over to someone she did not know. She worried that the ticket holder might take the gift card and not send the ticket. She messaged him a picture of the gift card with the first eight digits of the twelve-digit claim code showing. She said she would send the rest of the code once she had the ticket. "No sorry," messaged the ticket holder. "You sending all. Why you doubting? . . . I deal with trust."[26]

Desperate for the ticket, Fanning sent the last four digits of the gift card code. The seller thanked her and said he would email the ticket to her. Minutes ticked by without an email. Sensing that she was being scammed, Fanning tried to cancel the Amazon card, but it had already been used. "The scammer . . . used that time to fill up his Amazon cart before I could cancel the gift card, then deleted his Facebook profile before I was any the wiser,"[27] says Fanning.

Fanning could not believe that she had fallen for a social media scam. She later wrote:

I think when most people visualize Facebook-scamees, they picture older, computer-illiterate (if not well-meaning) Baby Boomers—not those who grew up with Facebook. Admittedly, I hadn't been all that active on Facebook the past few years. Despite my relative inactivity, I'm very Internet-savvy and grew up in the MTV Catfish generation, so I was well aware of the power of a reverse Google Images search and the red flags to look out for—until I wasn't.[28]

A Widespread Problem

Fanning was not the only victim of a social media scam in 2018. According to the Better Business Bureau (BBB), a nonprofit organization whose mission is to advance marketplace trust, 50,559 people reported being scammed on the internet in 2018. The average amount of money lost was $152. In 2019 the number of scam reports declined to 37,283, but the average loss increased to $160.

The scam with the most victims in 2018 involved online purchases like the one Fanning tried to make. The BBB received 10,240 reports of online purchase scams in 2018. Only 2.6 percent of online purchase scams involved event tickets, but that scam had the highest success rate: 88.8 percent. "It's gotten horrendously worse over the past year," says Noel Peters, a concert promoter and founder of Inertia Entertainment. "My recent show, I didn't look at the [Facebook] page for 24 hours and woke up to 60 scam posts."[29]

The scams did not always take place solely in social media. Many, like Fanning's ticket scam, involved a combination of social media and email. Other social media scams send the victims to websites, where they often fill out a form or application, giving the scammers valuable information. Fully 77 percent of the scams reported to the BBB in 2019 involved the internet in some way, with contact made through social media, websites, email, internet messaging (such as WhatsApp and Viber), and online classified ads. In 18.5 percent of the cases, the first contact was made through social media.

Some people think that only elderly people who are computer-illiterate fall victim to scams. In fact, people of all ages have been affected by social media trickery.

The IQ Scam

Social media scams succeed because they prey on common human weaknesses combined with a lack of critical thinking. Like fake news, some social media scams appeal to the ego of the reader and a desire to gain status within a group. Other scams appeal to the desire to find a dating partner. Others simply appeal to human greed.

One scam that appeals to the ego is the intelligence quotient (IQ) test. "Are you smarter than your friends?" asks one ad, playing on individuals' need to prove their intelligence. Sometimes a message that appears to come from a friend pops up and challenges the user to see who has the higher IQ. If the social media user clicks on the link to take the test, it usually opens a web page that features a series of questions. The page often has ads on it, so merely visiting the page helps the poster earn money from the advertisers, who pay a fee every time someone visits the page. Sometimes agreeing to take the test requires the victim to provide social media account information. The worst problem comes when users want to see the IQ test results. They often have to provide a phone number. The scammer then sells the phone number to a telemarketing company that bombards the social media user with sales calls.

> "[One scam] said Dave had taken an IQ test, gotten a score, see if you can beat him."[30]
>
> —Barb, phishing scam victim

A woman named Barb received an IQ challenge in a Facebook message. "It said Dave had taken an IQ test, gotten a score, see if you can beat him," Barb told CBS News. She found this intriguing. "I'm married to a Dave," she explains. However, the challenge had nothing to do with her husband. Barb had to provide her mobile phone number so she could receive a text with the test results. "And then the calls started,"[30] she says. She began receiving dozens of robotic sales calls, or robo calls.

Barb's experience was annoying, but others are more costly. The fine print at the bottom of the IQ test page sometimes says

Questionable Quizzes

How many people love and hate you? What type of men or women are you attracted to? What hair color suits your personality? These are all popular quiz questions widely shared on Facebook. On the surface, they appear harmless. But behind the fun some serious work is being done. Some quizzes are designed to harvest the user's personal information, according to the Better Business Bureau (BBB). The quizzes may ask what appear to be silly questions, but the people receiving the answers may be harvesting the personal information to build a profile of the users and even hack their social media account. Bill Fanelli, chief security officer at the BBB, explains, "We always knew someone was trying to trick us with social media quizzes because they are free. If there is no charge, then the value is the data they can collect. We also knew that it was for a use we probably would not like, because they went to such great lengths to hide their purpose. Now we know we were right on both counts." The BBB cautions users to pause before taking the quiz and try to figure out who is giving the quiz and if they are trustworthy.

Quoted in Joan Goodchild, "What Are the Seven Biggest Social Media Scams of 2018?," Security Intelligence, August 9, 2018. https://securityintelligence.com.

that the person agrees to subscribe to a cell phone service. The agreement is hidden in such a way that most people do not see it. In one scam, the IQ test takers subscribe to a text messaging service that charges $30 a month. In another, they sign up for a service for ring tones and other alerts that costs $9.99 a month. "They're really trying to steal your personal information, your cell phone number, so they can charge you," says Edgar Dworsky, a consumer advocate and founder of the consumer resource website Consumer World. "I think it's one of the worst Internet scams I've ever seen."[31]

Another scam that preys on users' personal pride or ego is the gossip scam. In this case the invitation usually offers to give the victim secret information about celebrities. The people who are being scammed often believe the information will put them "in the

> "[Scammers are] really trying to steal your personal information, your cell phone number, so they can charge you."[31]
>
> —Edgar Dworsky, consumer advocate

know" and above their peers, who do not have the same information. Gossip scams also play on readers' curiosity. The desire to gain the information can be particularly strong when the celebrity is someone the person being scammed admires. Clicking on these offers often takes people to a page that tells them that they must download a program such as Adobe Flash in order to read the juicy gossip. When users click "download" to proceed, they do not get the program they think they are getting. Instead, they are downloading malicious software, or "malware" for short—a program that is harmful to the operation of a computer. Once inside the computer, the malware can perform certain tasks, such as copying computer files and sending them back to the scammer. These files often contain personal information that the hacker can use to access the victim's accounts.

Gossip scams play on a reader's desire to get special insider information. When the reader is directed to click on an icon to get the scoop, they unknowingly download malware that hijacks their computer.

Phishing Scams

Not all scams work by playing on a user's desire to gain status. Some appeal to the user's fear of losing status. One such scam can originate in Facebook Messenger or Twitter messages. Sometimes the scammer hijacks a user's account and sends a message to that person's friends. The receivers of the message see their friend's profile picture and assume the message has come from that individual. Other times, the message is from an unknown person. In either case, the scammer pretends to have secret— often embarrassing—information about the person being scammed. One message asks, "Oh my god! Is this you in this photo?" The message contains a link to the apparently shocking photo. The link takes the user to a page that looks identical to a social media page. To see the picture, the victim must log in. If the person does so, the scammer will capture the user's log-in credentials, gaining access to the victim's account. This is known as a phishing scam. The scammer can sell or trade the victim's information to hackers or other cybercriminals on what is known as the dark web—computer networks that connect to the internet but require certain software or authorization to access. The hackers can then use the log-in credentials to send other scam messages to the user's friends.

A similar scam is the "see who viewed your profile" scam. This scam plays on people's curiosity by promising to allow them to find out who is secretly viewing their online profile. As with the "Is this you?" scam, the victim usually clicks a link that takes him or her to a facsimile of the social media website log-in page, where the scammer collects the victim's log-in credentials. The scammer can then log in to the account, change the password, and lock the victim out. The scammer can use the account to launch attacks on the victims' friends. Since scammer's messages appear to come from a social media friend, people receiving the messages are more likely to fall for the scam and become victims themselves.

Other common phishing scams play on fears of losing access to online accounts. Often delivered in social media messages,

 Our online services will be unavaila
9:00PM (ET) until Sunday August 2
again soon.

> Some of the most dangerous phishing scams send the victims to websites that mimic those of the Social Security Administration. These fake sites require the victims to enter their Social Security numbers.

 Learn How to Protect Your Social S

these scams suggest that the victim's access to a social media, email, photo storage, or streaming account has been suspended or soon will be. The person being scammed is asked to click on a link to resolve the problem. As in other phishing scams, the victim is taken to a page that duplicates the log-in page of a website. When the victim logs in to the fake site, the scammer obtains the victim's credentials to the real account.

Some of the most dangerous phishing scams send the victims to websites that mimic those of the Social Security Administration or another government agency. These fake sites require the victims to provide their Social Security number to proceed. Once scammers have a person's Social Security number, they are well on their way to stealing a person's identity. With a person's full name, Social Security number, birth date, and address, an identity thief often can open credit card accounts or take out loans in the victim's name. These phishing scams work because the fear of being locked out of important accounts temporarily overcomes the victim's usual skepticism and common sense.

Sometimes scammers satisfy their own greed by appealing to the greed of their victims. These scams offer something of value for free. The item can range from a Starbucks gift card to lottery winnings worth millions of dollars. Often, the fake offer will contain a time limit that says something like, "You only have 4 minutes and 15 seconds to claim your prize!" The time limit is designed to prompt action before the person has time to think through the offer. As with other phishing scams, clicking the link to claim the prize takes the victim to a fake page that looks official. The page usually asks for some kind personal identification to claim the prize. Some scams ask for a phone number to charge the victim for phone or data fees, as in the IQ scam. Lottery scams may require banking information so the purported winnings can be transferred to the victim's account. Instead, the scammer uses the bank information to steal money from the victim.

Catfishing

Many people who have been victimized for money or had their on-line accounts hijacked suffer embarrassment and emotional trauma. No one wants to appear as an easy "mark" for a con artist. But the worst feelings often are experienced by people who fall for a "catfish" scam. Catfishing is when a person creates a fake identity for the purpose of carrying on an online relationship. These individuals attract victims by posting profile pics of other, usually more attractive people to entice the victim into intimate chats. The victims of catfishing often form an emotional attachment to the person who is scamming them. As a result, the victims often experience heartbreak, loss, or shame when they discover that they have been fooled. The shame can be magnified if the victims have shared compromising pictures of themselves with the scammer.

Usually, catfishers only want to share intimacies with their victims, but in some cases they use the emotional attachment to

The willingness of social media scammers to exploit any tragedy for personal gain was once again on display during the COVID-19 pandemic. The FBI's Internet Crime Complaint Center reports that by April 21, 2020, it had received thirty-six hundred complaints related to COVID-19 scams, including posts for fraudulent vaccines, cures, and charity drives.

Some social media posts pretended to be linked to the Red Cross and other well-known relief agencies. Others provided links to apply for the federal government's COVID-19 stimulus payments in order to obtain banking details and other personal information. To attract traffic, the fake links often contained "covid19" or "coronavirus" in their addresses. "The department will continue to collaborate with our law enforcement and private sector partners to combat online COVID-19 related crime," says Assistant Attorney General Brian A. Benczkowski of the US Department of Justice's Criminal Division. "We commend the responsible internet companies that are taking swift action to prevent their resources from being used to exploit this pandemic." According to the Federal Trade Commission, Americans had lost nearly $12 million to COVID-19 scams by April 10, 2020.

Quoted in "Department of Justice Announces Disruption of Hundreds of Online COVID-19 Related Scams," *Justice News*, April 22, 2020. www.justice.gov.

bilk the victim out of gifts and money. According to the Federal Bureau of Investigation (FBI), Americans lost more than $474 million to romance scams in 2019. Whenever victims want to meet in person, the catfishers make up an excuse about why that is not possible. Sometimes they make the date but do not show up. The catfishers usually make up excuses about why they did not show up at the appointed time and place in hopes of continuing the scam.

Catfishing works because it plays on the human desire to find love. It also works because meeting people online has become commonplace. A 2019 study by Michael Rosenfeld and Sonia Hausen of Stanford University and Reuben Thomas of the University of New Mexico found that 39 percent of heterosexual couples and 60 percent of same-sex couples met online. More people meet online than in any other way. Because online relationships are not unusual, many people find themselves trusting people they have never met in person. Catfishers know this and exploit it for their own benefit.

An attractive partner, easy money, the satisfaction of being ahead of one's peers—these are things that appeal to almost everyone. Most people logically know things of value do not come easily, but the dangers of taking a quiz or answering a greeting from an attractive stranger are well hidden behind the engaging qualities of social media. As a result, people find themselves doing things on social media that they would never do in person, including falling for scams and giving their private information to a total stranger.

Chapter Three

Medical Hoaxes

People have a great interest in their personal health and in the health and well-being of those near to them. Knowing that the internet is packed with information, 80 percent of internet users search for health-related information online, according to a 2018 survey by Doctors.com. Websites run by Healthline Media, WebMD, the Mayo Clinic, and the National Institutes of Health provide scientifically accurate medical information to about 250 million visitors each month.

Unfortunately, less reliable organizations are providing a great deal of false and misleading health information on the internet. A 2018 study by researchers at Medical University of Gdansk in Poland found that 40 percent of the most-shared social media links about common diseases contain misinformation. A December 2019 study by NBC News analyzed eighty of the most-shared social media articles on health topics, all of which had twenty-five thousand shares or more. In the case of some topics, including cancer and fluoride, there were more fake health stories than legitimate ones. Medical fakery is rampant in social media.

Cancer Cons

NBC News found that about a third of all false medical stories promote unproven cures for cancer. The focus on cancer is not surprising. It is the second-leading cause of death in the United States, according to the Centers for Disease Control and Prevention, the US agency charged with tracking and investigating public health trends. In addition, cancer is a mysterious disease, consisting of more than one hundred different types, including breast cancer, skin cancer, lung cancer, colon cancer, prostate cancer, and lymphoma.

Cancer is notoriously difficult to cure. About 67 percent of people treated for cancer survive for five years or more, but 33 percent do not. The survival rate varies greatly, depending on which cancer a person has developed. For example, 98 percent of people diagnosed with thyroid cancer survive for five years or more after treatment, but only 6 percent of people with pancreatic cancer live that long. The life-and-death stakes of cancer treatment cause some people, desperate for a cure, to pursue alternative treatments that have not been proved safe and effective by the scientific methods used by the medical establishment.

Traditional cancer treatment can be long and painful, and this also motivates cancer patients to search for alternatives. Traditional cancer treatment often includes surgery to remove the cancerous growth, or tumor. It can also involve radiation therapy, which uses high-energy radiation such as X-rays and gamma rays to shrink tumors and kill cancer cells. Cancer treatment often involves chemotherapy, which uses toxic chemicals to destroy the cancer cells. All these treatments can have serious side effects, including pain, nausea, fatigue, and emotional distress. That is why alternative treatments that do not cause such side effects intrigue many cancer patients, making the patients, their friends, and family vulnerable to unproven claims.

Many alternative cancer treatments involve dietary supplements. "Ginger is 10,000x more effective at killing cancer than chemo,"[32] reads the headline of a social media article that generated more than eight hundred thousand engagements, according to NBC News. "Black Garlic Is Toxic to 14 Types of Cancer,"[33] states an article linked to by the Facebook group Old Natural Cures. "The New Super Mushroom Tea That Can Destroy Cancer

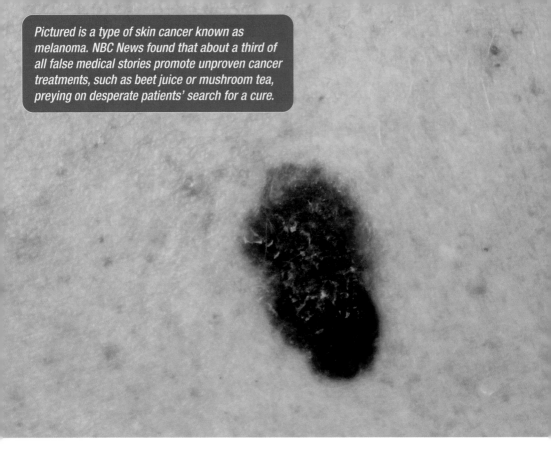

Cells Yet Is Gentle on the Digestive System,"[34] begins another post on the Old Natural Cures site. Papaya leaf, beet juice, moringa leaf, alkaline water, and other fruits, vegetables, herbs, and liquids are all touted as cures for cancer despite the fact that they have not been proved safe and effective by the US Food and Drug Administration (FDA) or any other scientific organization. Not surprisingly, the ads on the same pages as these posts, as well as the websites the articles link to, often sell the miracle substances being promoted as cures.

Marijuana Misdirection

The most popular alternative treatment for cancer is marijuana, according to a 2019 study by researchers at Stanford University. The researchers found that online searches for cancer and marijuana grew at ten times the rate of searches for traditional medical treatment. A non-intoxicating marijuana extract known as cannabidiol (CBD) has been approved by the FDA for the treatment of two childhood epilepsy syndromes. However, it has not been shown to be safe or effective for the treatment of cancer. Nevertheless, many social media posts promote CBD as a miracle cure for cancer. Typically, these stories link to websites that sell CBD. Legal in forty-seven states and the District of Columbia, CBD is big business.

Some social media posters not only hype CBD and other marijuana products, they also seek to undermine confidence in traditional medicine. "Cancer industry not looking for a cure; they're too busy making money,"[35] states a September 2019 social media post that attracted 5.4 million visits to Natural News, a website owned and operated by Mike Adams, a seller of dietary supplements. The post suggests that an indifference toward death exists among those who are charged with preventing it.

A similar message appears in an article that an October 2019 post on the Facebook page of Natural Cancer Cures links to: "Over a Million People DIE from Chemotherapy Every Year, but Only 750,000 Pass Away from Cancer—What's WRONG with This Picture?"[36] The article, which appears on the Natural News website, goes on to attack the American Medical Association (AMA), the largest association of physicians and medical students in the United States: "Chemical warfare on humanity was launched nearly a century ago by the American Medical Association, when they eliminated nutrition classes from medical colleges and approval-stamped any chemical medication that came down the pike as the drug of choice for whatever ailment any doctor chose to manage for their 'patients for life.'"[37]

Criticizing the AMA and the pharmaceutical industry plays on the desire of some people to be part of an elite, informed group—people who are smarter than the medical establishment and who refuse to be manipulated by it. Such posts are designed to create confusion and make people doubt the value of traditional medicine—a condition that benefits sellers of ingredients for home remedies, dietary supplements, and alternative medicines.

The non-intoxicating extracts of marijuana are not the only parts of the plant that are being promoted for cancer treatment. Smoking the intoxicating leaves and flower buds are also touted as a cure for cancer. Comedian Tommy Chong, who was diagnosed with prostate cancer in 2012, claims he defeated his disease with the help of marijuana: "So the magic plant does cure cancer with the right diet and supplements,"[38] he says. Chong and others are frequently quoted in social media, extolling the medical benefits of smoking marijuana.

Comedian Tommy Chong (pictured) claims he defeated prostate cancer, in part, by smoking marijuana. Chong and others are frequently quoted in social media extolling the medical benefits of marijuana and THC.

Hyping the unproven medical benefits of marijuana that contains THC, the intoxicating compound found in the drug, is part of a strategy to legalize recreational marijuana, says author Alex Berenson. "The cannabis advocacy community has done everything possible to confuse the way medical legalization works in practice," says Berenson. "Marijuana is not 'prescribed' for anything. It can't be, because the FDA has never approved it to treat any disease, and there is little evidence that smoked cannabis or THC extracts help [treat] any . . . diseases."[39] Although the benefits of smoked marijuana are unproven, thirty-three state legislatures have legalized its use to treat a range of medical disorders, including nausea associated with chemotherapy, glaucoma, HIV/AIDS, Huntington's disease, and Parkinson's disease.

"The cannabis advocacy community has done everything possible to confuse the way medical legalization works in practice."[39]

—Alex Berenson, author

The strategy of associating even smoked marijuana with medical benefits is paying off for the marijuana industry. Since 2015 twelve states and the District of Columbia have legalized the sale and consumption of marijuana for recreational purposes. Legal marijuana sales in the United States topped $10 billion in 2018.

Dangerous Quackery

Although marijuana products—especially those with high concentrations of THC—can have dangerous side effects, including anxiety, panic attacks, and short-term psychosis, they usually are safe for adults when used in moderation. They may not cure cancer, but they usually will not harm the adult user. The same is true of ginger, beet root juice, and other natural remedies. However, one alleged skin cancer treatment is dangerous: black salve. Most black salves are made from bloodroot, a plant that contains a toxic chemical that destroys living tissue—sanguinarine. In the late nineteenth and early twentieth centuries, doctors used black salve to treat skin lesions, but the FDA does not approve the use of the topical paste for any medical purpose. In fact, the FDA lists black salve as one of 187 fake cancer cures that consumers should avoid. "Things like black salve just kill everything, normal skin cells, abnormal skin cells, it doesn't matter," says Douglas Grose, president of the Cosmetic Physicians College of Australasia. "You can't control it. All you're doing is killing the full thickness of the skin and allowing it to scar up. It's a ridiculous technique."[40]

Despite the FDA's warning, several Facebook pages promote black salve as a cancer treatment. These pages include Black Salve Alliance, Bloodroot Black Salves, and Cancer Cures. An April 2020 testimonial on the Black Salve Alliance page shows how important the campaign against traditional medicine is to the promotion of alternative remedies. "Great Natural Product that WORKS," reads the post. "Big Pharma afraid of this natural healer."[41] Another April 2020 post on the same page illustrates how alternative medicine purveyors appeal to the potential customer's ego and desire to belong to an informed elite. "Independent thinkers not subscribing to mass destruction,"[42] proclaims the post. The Cancer Cures page links to an article that uses the medical establishment's condemnations of black salve as a selling point:

> Black Salve has been dubbed "dangerous" by Medical authorities—for example, the FDA has listed it as a "fake cancer treatment" since 2004; in Australia the Therapeutic Goods Administration condemned the ointment in 2012. However, its use in Australia is thought to be widespread. One Australian Doctor told a patient with Skin cancer "You might as well pour acid on it."[43]

Hidden Dangers

Getting people to use a harmful substance like black salve is an obvious danger of medical misinformation promoted in social media. Another, less obvious danger is that people who use an alternative treatment often refuse or avoid a traditional one that might save their lives. A 2017 study published in the *Journal of the National Cancer Institute* found that cancer patients who used only alternative medicine were two and a half times more likely to die during a five-year period than were patients who used standard cancer treatments such as surgery, radiation, and chemotherapy.

There is no way to know how many people die each year from the negative effects of alternative medicines. That is because few clinical trials of alternative treatments are conducted. In a clinical trial, which is required by the FDA before a new drug can be prescribed for treatment, the substance is given to patients to see how effective it is. At the same time, the side effects of the drug are carefully documented and analyzed. Since no records are kept for alternative treatments, their negative effects are unknown. "The vast majority of alternative therapies either haven't been rigorously studied or haven't been found to benefit patients,"[44] says Dr. Richard Schilsky, chief medical officer for the American Society of

> "The vast majority of alternative therapies either haven't been rigorously studied or haven't been found to benefit patients."[44]
>
> —Dr. Richard Schilsky, chief medical officer for the American Society of Clinical Oncology

Clinical Oncology, a leading group of cancer doctors. Nevertheless, a whopping 40 percent of Americans believe that cancer can be cured solely through alternative therapies, according to a 2018 survey conducted by the American Society of Clinical Oncology.

Immunizing the Public Against Vaccines

Some medical hoaxes do damage by convincing people to use a dangerous natural remedy like black salve. Other hoaxes cause harm by convincing people to use alternative treatments instead of traditional ones. There is a third kind of social media medical misinformation: social media pages and posts that encourage people to avoid vaccines.

First popularized by eighteenth-century English doctor Edward Jenner, who infected patients with cowpox to protect them against the deadlier smallpox, vaccines introduce a biological preparation similar to a particular virus or bacteria into the body to prepare the immune system to fight against the real, more dangerous pathogen. Widespread vaccination prevents a disease from spreading through a population, because the pathogen is unable to find a new host and eventually dies off. Global use of the smallpox vaccine led to smallpox being eradicated in 1980. Since the 1950s the continued use of a vaccine has nearly eradicated polio, a disease that infects the spinal cord and can cause paralysis and death. In 2015 the World Health Organization (WHO) announced that type 2 poliovirus had been eradicated, and in 2019 WHO announced that type 3 poliovirus had also been eradicated. Only type 1 poliovirus remains, and it causes only about five hundred new cases per year worldwide. According to WHO, vaccines prevent 2 million to 3 million deaths a year. Wider use of vaccines could save another 1.5 million lives every year.

In the United States state laws require schoolchildren to be vaccinated against common diseases, including measles, mumps, rubella, diphtheria, tetanus, pertussis, polio, and chicken pox. These laws often apply to children attending public schools, private schools, and day care facilities. Because of these policies, most of the diseases on the state immunization lists have nearly been eradicated in the United States. Vaccines are constantly being developed to fight new diseases. When the coronavirus emerged in 2019, governments around the world announced a series of policies designed to slow the spread of the virus until a vaccine could be developed against it.

Not everyone supports the policy of mandating vaccinations. Some people object on religious grounds. For example, some Christian Scientists, who normally rely on prayer for healing, prefer not to be vaccinated, although the church does not forbid vaccination. Other religious people object to using vaccines that are made by growing viruses in cells originally obtained from aborted fetuses. As a result, forty-five states allow vaccination exemptions on religious grounds. Another fifteen states allow vaccination exemptions based on philosophical or personal beliefs. The number of people in this last category is growing, in part because of deceptive posts on social media.

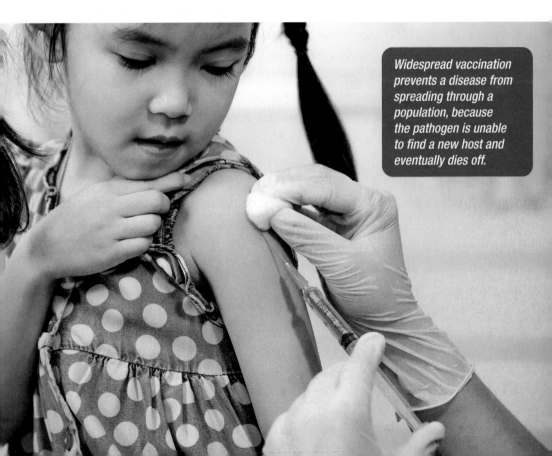

Widespread vaccination prevents a disease from spreading through a population, because the pathogen is unable to find a new host and eventually dies off.

Groups like Natural News, Children's Health Defense, and Stop Mandatory Vaccination use social media to promote vaccine hesitancy, a reluctance or refusal to receive a vaccine or to have one's children vaccinated against contagious diseases. In 2019 the anti-vaccine messages of these three groups generated more than a million engagements on social media, according to NBC News. In 2019 WHO identified vaccine hesitancy as one of the top ten global health threats of 2019.

Vaccination has had critics ever since Jenner introduced the concept in the eighteenth century, but the recent anti-vaccination movement gained momentum in 1998, when Andrew Wakefield, a researcher at Royal Free Hospital School of Medicine in London, and twelve of his colleagues published a paper in the medical journal the *Lancet* that linked the measles, mumps, and rubella (MMR) vaccine to behavioral regression and autism. The paper received wide publicity, and MMR vaccination rates began to drop because parents were concerned about the risk of autism after vaccination.

Numerous follow-up medical studies found no link between vaccines and autism, and in February 2010 the *Lancet* completely retracted the Wakefield paper, admitting that several elements in the paper were incorrect. An investigation by noted medical journal the *BMJ* later found that Wakefield and his colleagues were guilty of deliberate fraud. The investigation found that the researchers had presented only the data that supported their case. They had even falsified some results. Nevertheless, high-profile celebrities like actress Jenny McCarthy, actor Robert De Niro, and activist Robert F. Kennedy Jr., are leading a crusade against vaccinations. According to a January 2020 study published in the medical journal *Vaccine*, Kennedy's World Mercury Project was behind 54 percent of the 145 anti-vaccine advertisements that ran on Facebook from May 31, 2017, to February 22, 2019. The anti-vaccination activists, or anti-vaxxers, claim that the rise of autism diagnoses coincides with a more aggressive vaccination schedule for children in the United States.

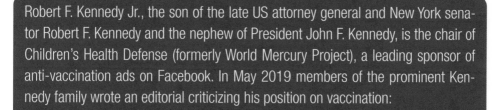

Robert F. Kennedy Jr.'s Family Criticizes His Anti-Vaccine Work

Robert F. Kennedy Jr., the son of the late US attorney general and New York senator Robert F. Kennedy and the nephew of President John F. Kennedy, is the chair of Children's Health Defense (formerly World Mercury Project), a leading sponsor of anti-vaccination ads on Facebook. In May 2019 members of the prominent Kennedy family wrote an editorial criticizing his position on vaccination:

> The WHO, the health arm of the United Nations, has listed vaccine hesitancy as one of the top 10 threats to global health in 2019. Most cases of preventable diseases occur among unvaccinated children, because parents have chosen not to vaccinate, have delayed vaccination, have difficulty accessing vaccines, or the children were too young to receive the vaccines.

> These tragic numbers are caused by the growing fear and mistrust of vaccines—amplified by internet doomsayers. Robert F. Kennedy Jr.—Joe and Kathleen's brother and Maeve's uncle—is part of this campaign to attack the institutions committed to reducing the tragedy of preventable infectious diseases. He has helped to spread dangerous misinformation over social media and is complicit in sowing distrust of the science behind vaccines.

> We love Bobby. He is one of the great champions of the environment. . . . We stand behind him in his ongoing fight to protect our environment. However, on vaccines he is wrong.

Kathleen Kennedy Townsend, Joseph P. Kennedy II, and Maeve Kennedy McKean, "RFK Jr. Is Our Brother and Uncle. He's Tragically Wrong About Vaccines," *Politico*, May 8, 2019. www.politico.com.

The anti-vaxxers often use deceptive arguments to bolster their unproven claims. For example, Stop Mandatory Vaccination often promotes articles by grieving parents who claim that their babies' deaths were the result of a vaccination, rather than the causes found by official medical examiners, including sudden infant death syndrome, pneumonia, and accidental asphyxiation. California state senator Richard Pan, a pediatrician, denounces the tactic. "It's one thing for a family to say, 'My child died,'" Pan says. "But when you say, 'It was caused by vaccines, and now I want to change laws or stop laws in a way that will hurt children,' then it's not inappropriate to say: 'Where's the proof?'"[45]

It is natural for grieving family members to want to find out why their loved ones have died or developed a disorder. These feelings have been the impetus behind many medical discoveries over the centuries. The search for answers and the desire to spare other people from the trauma that one's own family has experienced can blind some people to scientific facts and make them vulnerable to medical hoaxes. Social media scammers know this and are willing to exploit these vulnerabilities for their own gain.

Chapter Four

Combating Social Media Falsehoods

When David Acke, a reporter from the Belgian newspaper *Het Laatste Nieuws*, interviewed Kris Van Kerckhoven, a doctor with a practice near Antwerp, Belgium, in January 2020, the COVID-19 pandemic had barely started. Only nine people were thought to have died from the disease, almost all of them in Wuhan, China. Acke noted that several 5G cell phone towers had been built around Wuhan before the outbreak. He asked Van Kerckhoven if there could be any connection between the two things. "I have not done a fact check," said Van Kerckhoven. "But it may be a link with current events."[46] That was all the newspaper needed. It put a subhead reading "Link with coronavirus" above the quote and titled the article "5G is life-threatening, and no one knows it."[47]

The 5G Hoax

Simon Clarke, an associate professor in cellular microbiology at the University of Reading in England, says there is no scientific reason to link 5G networks and the coronavirus. "The idea that Covid-19 is caused by 5G mobile phone signals is complete rubbish," says Clarke. "5G radio signals are electromagnetic waves, very similar to those already used by mobile phones. Electromagnetic waves are one thing, viruses are another, and you can't get a virus off a phone mast."[48] *Het Laatste Nieuws* quickly pulled the baseless story from its website. "Because the quotes were unfounded, we withdrew the article within a few hours," says Dimitri Antonissen, the newspaper's editor. "We regret the fact that the story was online for a few hours."[49] In another era, that might have been the end of the story, but in the age of social media, it was only getting started.

As far back as the 1990s, conspiracy theorists have argued that cell phone signals are dangerous. The story in *Het Laatste Nieuws* gave new energy to the old beliefs. Anti-5G Facebook pages in the Dutch-speaking world quoted the article and linked to it. Within days the story had spread to the English-speaking world, popping up on Facebook, Twitter, and YouTube. Although seen by thousands, the 5G conspiracy theory maintained a relatively low profile until celebrities got into the act. Actors Woody Harrelson and John Cusack, singers M.I.A. and Anne-Marie, pop star Keri Hilson, boxer Amir Khan, and British television stars Lucy Watson and Amanda Holden all tweeted about the fringe belief, bringing it to the attention of millions. Holden even tweeted a link to a Change.org petition that claimed that the symptoms of exposure to 5G are very much like the symptoms of coronavirus. In April 2020 anti-5G sentiments came to a boil. At least twenty mobile phone masts were vandalized across England, and several were set on fire.

Censoring Incitement

Seeing the role social media had played in promoting the 5G conspiracy theory, Facebook and Twitter decided to act. Facebook blocked two anti-5G groups: Stop 5G UK and Destroy 5G Save Our Children. Stop 5G UK had about sixty thousand members. Destroy 5G Save Our Children had about twenty-five hundred members. Facebook declared:

Content encouraging attacks on 5G masts clearly violates our policies and we have removed a number of Pages, Groups and posts. Over the last week, under our existing policies against harmful misinformation, we have also begun removing false claims that 5G technology causes the symptoms of or contraction of COVID-19. We will continue to work closely with governments, other tech companies and third parties to remove harmful misinformation and promote official guidance from local health authorities.[50]

A Conspiracy Theory Goes Viral

A conspiracy theory can spread through social media like wildfire. On January 22, 2020, a Belgian newspaper reported the conspiracy theory that COVID-19 was being spread by 5G mobile phone towers. The theory received few mentions on social media until April 3, 2020, when the number of daily mentions tripled from twenty thousand to sixty thousand. The mentions increased by another 50 percent by April 6, reaching a peak of eighty-five thousand in one day. The mentions continued in the tens of thousands thereafter. The graph was developed by analyzing public posts on Twitter, Facebook, and other online forums.

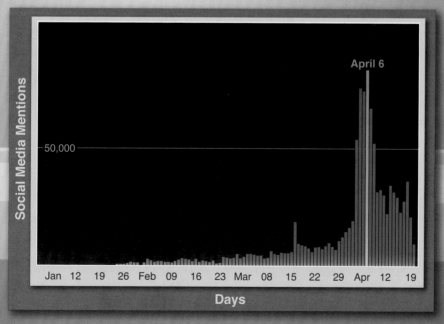

Source: Rebecca Heilweil, "How the 5G Coronavirus Conspiracy Theory Went from Finge to Mainstream," Vox, April 24, 2020. www.vox.com/recode/2020/4/24/21231085/coronavirus-5g-conspiracy-theory-covid-facebook-youtube.

Twitter also announced that it would remove any tweets calling for people to disrupt 5G networks. "We have broadened our guidance on unverified claims that incite people to engage in harmful activity, could lead to the destruction or damage of critical 5G infrastructure, or could lead to widespread panic, social unrest, or large-scale disorder,"[51] the company tweeted on April 22, 2020. Twitter announced that it had removed more than 2,230 tweets containing misleading and potentially harmful content.

Facebook and Twitter also announced restrictions on fake news regarding the COVID-19 pandemic apart from the 5G hoax. Twitter said it would ban statements that incited people to hoard food and other supplies. "Our automated systems have challenged more than 3.4 million accounts targeting manipulative dis-

Is the 5G Hoax a Disinformation Campaign?

Rumors linking 5G cellular networks to the outbreak of COVID-19 sped through social media with mind-boggling speed. Most experts assumed that the fake news story was spread by uncritical conspiracy theorists, from its first mention in a Belgian newspaper until it was amplified by Hollywood celebrities. However, Marc Owen Jones, a researcher at Hamad Bin Khalifa University in Doha, Qatar, believes the spread of the 5G story may have been the result of a coordinated disinformation campaign.

An expert in online disinformation networks, Jones analyzed twenty-two thousand tweets, retweets, and comments mentioning "5G" and "corona." He found a large number of Twitter accounts displaying what he calls "inauthentic activity," including automated posts by robots, or bots. "There are very strong indications that some of these accounts are a disinformation operation," Jones says. The pattern of activity resembles the operation conducted by Russia's Internet Research Agency during the 2016 US presidential campaign. However, Jones has not yet concluded whether Russia or any other nation is behind the 5G disinformation campaign.

Quoted in Ryan Gallagher, "5G Virus Conspiracy Theory Fueled by Coordinated Effort," Bloomberg, April 9, 2020. www.bloomberg.com.

cussions around COVID-19,"[52] Twitter announced in April 2020.

Similarly, Facebook took action against organizations that promoted anti-lockdown protests during the COVID-19 pandemic. These protesters argued that it was time to lift restrictions on people's movements and activities. Discussing the issue on social media was permitted, but calling for people to violate lockdown orders by assembling in groups was not.

Silencing Anti-Vaxxers

Facebook has taken a similar position toward anti-vaccine misinformation. In March 2019 the company announced that it would reduce the news feed and search rankings of groups and pages that spread misinformation about vaccinations. The company also said it would reject ads that include misinformation about vaccinations. If an advertiser continued to violate the new policies, its account might be suspended. In April 2019 Facebook added that it would remove access to its fundraising tools for pages that spread misinformation about vaccinations. "We are working to tackle vaccine misinformation on Facebook by reducing its distribution and providing people with authoritative information on the topic,"[53] says Monika Bickert, vice president of Facebook's global policy management.

> "We are working to tackle vaccine misinformation on Facebook by reducing its distribution and providing people with authoritative information on the topic."[53]
>
> —Monika Bickert, vice president of Facebook's global policy management

Other social media outlets are also taking action against anti-vaccine messages. YouTube does not allow ads to appear on videos that promote anti-vaccination content. As a result, groups posting the videos cannot make money through advertising. Pinterest, which allows users to save and discover images, GIFs, and videos on the internet, does not allow users to link to websites that have vaccine misinformation. "We're a place to go to for inspiration, and there's nothing inspiring about harmful content,"[54] says Ifeoma Ozoma, Pinterest's policy and social impact manager.

Automated Policing

Because social media is so widespread, with billions of users worldwide, the social media companies use computers to police their networks for misinformation. The computers employ a process known as supervised machine learning to evaluate posts and comments. In this process the computer is told exactly what patterns of data—words, numbers, images, and links—it should look for. It is like giving a bloodhound or a drug-sniffing dog a scent to search for. The computer then processes huge amounts of data, searching for the target patterns. When it finds them, it flags them, according to the rules each company has put into place.

Automated systems can identify some deceptive ads and posts, but some experts do not believe that this method of policing social media can remove all misinformation. They point out that the same technological tools and techniques that are being used to find and block misinformation can be used by bad actors to disguise it. "Machine learning and sophisticated statistical techniques will be used to accurately simulate real information content and make fake information almost indistinguishable from the real thing,"[55] says Scott Spangler, principal data scientist at IBM Watson Health. Another problem is the huge volume of data in all social media. Some experts believe that the attack surface—the amount of data being posted on social media platforms and the speed at which it is being generated—is too large to be successfully policed even with automated systems.

The Future of Fake News

In 2017 the Pew Research Center surveyed 1,116 communications experts about social media deception. The researchers asked whether in the next ten years the information environment will be "improved" or "not be improved" by changes that reduce the spread of lies and other misinformation online. The experts were split. Forty-nine percent said the information environment will improve; 51 percent said it will not improve. Those who said the situation will improve tended to point to history as evidence that human beings have a drive to fix problems and that technology usually enables such improvements. Those who said the situation will not improve pointed out that the main motivations behind social media deception—greed and the desire for power—are more powerful incentives than those behind improving the information environment, and that these incentives will cause bad actors to outwit and outwork those who are trying to police them. "Things will not improve," says Stephen Downes, a researcher with the National Research Council Canada. "There is too much incentive to spread disinformation, fake news, malware and the rest."[56]

> "Things will not improve. There is too much incentive to spread disinformation, fake news, malware and the rest."[56]
>
> —Stephen Downes, researcher with the National Research Council Canada

Amber Case, a research fellow at Harvard University's Berkman Klein Center for Internet & Society, disagrees. She believes that financial incentives can be used to clean up the social media environment. "Right now, there is an incentive to spread fake news. It is profitable to do so, profit made by creating an article that causes enough outrage that advertising money will follow," Case

YouTube does not allow ads to appear on videos that promote anti-vaccination content. This discourages groups from posting the videos because they will not receive any advertising revenue.

explains. She recommends holding back the advertising funds earned by a page, video, or other social media post until the content of the post is found to be true. "If an article bursts into collective consciousness and is later proven to be fake, the sites that control or host that content could refuse to distribute advertising revenue to the entity that created or published it," she says. "A lot of fake news is created by a few people, and removing their incentive could stop much of the news postings."[57]

Not all bad actors are motivated by the desire for money, however. Some are motivated by a lust for power. These are often the business and political leaders who should be calling for change. Instead, they have a stake in keeping things as they are. "So many players and interests see online information as a uniquely powerful shaper of individual action and public opinion in ways that serve their economic or political interests," says Leah Lievrouw, a professor in the Department of Information Studies at the University of California, Los Angeles. "These very diverse players would likely oppose (or try to subvert) technological or policy interventions or other attempts to insure the quality, and especially the disinterestedness, of information."[58]

Social Media and Free Speech

A major barrier to curbing social media deception in the United States is the country's history of protecting free speech rights. The underlying theory of free speech is that truth will triumph over falsehood when both sides are allowed to participate in a free and open debate. "If there be time to expose through discussion the falsehood and fallacies, to avert the evil by the processes of education, the remedy to be applied is more speech, not enforced silence,"[59] declared Supreme Court justice Louis D. Brandeis in the 1927 case *Whitney v. California*. "The answer to vicious or wrongheaded speech is always more speech, com-

During the COVID-19 pandemic, Facebook banned posts promoting demonstrations against social distancing policies. Facebook founder Mark Zuckerberg (pictured) appeared on ABC News to explain that the purpose of the ban was to discourage illegal behavior.

pelling speech, persuasive speech,"[60] says John Frohnmayer, a former chair of the National Endowment for the Arts. Under this scenario, social media platforms should not attempt to silence any ideas. They should remain a forum for all sides to be heard.

The problem with this scenario is that people using social media are not listening to all sides. For the most part, they listen to the side they agree with, and they do not spend much time evaluating whether it is true. Nevertheless, removing false information will be criticized as censorship, and social media companies do not want to be seen as censors. For example, when Facebook banned posts calling for demonstrations in violation of state social distancing policies, Facebook founder Mark Zuckerberg drew a distinction between limiting the discussion of ideas, which most people would consider censorship, and banning speech that incites lawless actions. "It's important that people can debate policies, so there's a line on this," Zuckerberg told ABC News anchor George Stephanopoulos. "But more than normal political discourse, I think

After Facebook shut down pages of groups that were organizing demonstrations against the COVID-19 lockdown, Kalev Leetaru, a senior fellow at the George Washington University Center for Cyber and Homeland Security, reflected on the move:

> [Facebook] is no longer just a place for friends to share family photos and chat online. It is now the de facto town square through which democratic societies communicate with their elected officials and organize demonstrations when they feel those officials no longer represent their interests.
>
> That a private company can now unilaterally decide to simply delete the promotion of protests it deems unacceptable is a remarkable expansion of its power over what was once a sacrosanct and constitutionally protected freedom. As we cede the public square to private companies, however, those constitutional freedoms of speech and expression no longer apply in some cases. Through those private companies, in fact, government officials can in effect restrict speech they are obligated to protect. . . .
>
> In the end, while we might question the wisdom of crowded protests in the midst of a pandemic, the responsibility for curbing such actions must fall to democratically elected governments answerable to the people, not private companies accountable to no one.

Kalev Leetaru, "Facebook's COVID-Protest Ban Renews Censorship Concerns," RealClearPolitics, April 22, 2020. www.realclearpolitics.com.

a lot of the stuff that people are saying that is false around a health emergency like this can be classified as harmful misinformation."[61]

The free flow of ideas—good and bad, true and untrue—probably will not be limited by social media platforms. "Misinformation will continue to thrive because of the long (and valuable) tradition of freedom of expression," says one academic. "Censorship will be rejected."[62]

A final barrier to eliminating social media deception is one that has plagued thinkers from the beginning of time: how to distinguish truth from falsehood. Two people—even if they both have good intentions—can look at the same thing and see it differently. One may think it is true, and the other may think it is false. In addition, factual information can be arranged in a way that creates a false impression or conclusion. If distinguishing between truth and falsehood is difficult for people, there is little hope that machines can do better. "'Fake' and 'true' are not as binary as we would like," says a research assistant at MIT, "and—combined with an increasingly connected and complex digital society—it's a challenge to manage the complexity of social media without prescribing a narrative as 'truth.'"[63]

Because of the barriers to counteracting social media deception, it is likely to remain a problem far into the future. Perhaps the most important thing is for social media users to be aware of how misinformation can shape their opinions and to use critical thinking to keep their minds from being hijacked by bad actors.

Introduction: A Crisis of Truth

1. Quoted in Janna Anderson and Lee Rainie, "The Future of Truth and Misinformation Online," Pew Research Center, October 19, 2017. www.pewresearch.org.
2. Quoted in Anderson and Rainie, "The Future of Truth and Misinformation Online."
3. Quoted in Anderson and Rainie, "The Future of Truth and Misinformation Online."

Chapter One: Deception and Distrust

4. John Duca, "This is from a immunologist at Johns Hopkins University," Facebook, March 19, 2020. www.facebook.com/john.duca.10/posts/3378539675494255.
5. Quoted in Duca, "This is from a immunologist at Johns Hopkins University."
6. Quoted in Duca, "This is from a immunologist at Johns Hopkins University."
7. Quoted in Ed Yong, "Why the Coronavirus Has Been So Successful," *The Atlantic*, March 20, 2020. www.theatlantic.com.
8. Quoted in Yong, "Why the Coronavirus Has Been So Successful."
9. Quoted in Alex Kasprak, "'Good Read from an Immunologist' Post Misstates Reasons for COVID-19's Virulence," Snopes, March 23, 2020. www.snopes.com.
10. McHugh David, "Harvard Professor Explains Importance Social Distancing, 'Flattening the Curve,'" *Livingston Parish News* (Denham Springs, LA), March 18, 2020. www.livingstonparishnews.com.
11. wombat 5606, "Saw something the other day that I agree with," DIS Boards, March 18, 2020. www.disboards.com/threads/carnival-vs-dcl-the-discussion-and-comparison-thread.3540991/page-234#post-61691478.
12. Eileen H, "How We Got Here, Why Covid19 Is NOT like Seasonal Flu and Why the Measures Matter," Patient, March 15, 2020. https://patient.info.

13. LaBamba, "What Makes Covid-19 Scarier to You than Swine Flu or Ebola?," Lipstick Alley, March 18, 2020. www.lipstickalley.com.

14. Quoted in LaBamba, "What Makes Covid-19 Scarier to You than Swine Flu or Ebola?"

15. Quoted in LaBamba, "What Makes Covid-19 Scarier to You than Swine Flu or Ebola?"

16. Quoted in LaBamba, "What Makes Covid-19 Scarier to You than Swine Flu or Ebola?"

17. Quoted in LaBamba, "What Makes Covid-19 Scarier to You than Swine Flu or Ebola?"

18. Quoted in LaBamba, "What Makes Covid-19 Scarier to You than Swine Flu or Ebola?"

19. Quoted in Institute of Humane Studies, "Social Media, Tribalism, and the Prevalence of Fake News," *Big Think* (blog), June 12, 2019. https://theihs.org.

20. Quoted in Anderson and Rainie, "The Future of Truth and Misinformation Online."

21. Quoted in Anderson and Rainie, "The Future of Truth and Misinformation Online."

22. Quoted in John C. Moritz, "Facebook Ads: Russians Targeted Texas Secessionist Movement, Ripped Hillary Clinton," *USA Today*, May 10, 2018. www.usatoday.com.

23. Quoted in Moritz, "Facebook Ads."

24. Quoted in Jeremy Herb and Zachary Cohen, "Bipartisan Senate Report Backs Intel Community Assessment That Russia Interfered to Help Trump in 2016 Election," CNN, April 21, 2020. www.cnn.com.

25. Quoted in Mary Clare Jalonick and Eric Tucker, "Bipartisan Senate Report Backs Assessment That Russia Interfered in the 2016 Presidential Election," *Time*, April 21, 2020. https://time.com.

Chapter Two: Falling for Scams

26. Quoted in Caroline Fanning, "I Got Scammed on Facebook—Here's What I Learned," *Reader's Digest*, February 20, 2020. www.rd.com.

27. Fanning, "I Got Scammed on Facebook—Here's What I Learned."

28. Fanning, "I Got Scammed on Facebook—Here's What I Learned."

29. Quoted in Fanning, "I Got Scammed on Facebook—Here's What I Learned."

30. Quoted in David Wade, "Curious About Facebook 'IQ Test Scams,'" CBS Boston, October 1, 2010. https://boston.cbslocal.com.

31. Quoted in Wade, "Curious About Facebook 'IQ Test Scams.'"

Chapter Three: Medical Hoaxes

32. Quoted in Brandy Zadrozny, "Social Media Hosted a Lot of Fake Health News This Year. Here's What Went Most Viral," NBC News, December 29, 2019. www.nbcnews.com.
33. Ivana Saragjinova, "Black Garlic Is Toxic to 14 Types of Cancer," Old Natural Cures, April 4, 2019. www.oldnaturalcures.com.
34. "The New Super Mushroom Tea That Can Destroy Cancer Cells Yet Is Gentle on the Digestive System," Old Natural Cures, April 17, 2020. www.oldnaturalcures.com.
35. Quoted in Zadrozny, "Social Media Hosted a Lot of Fake Health News This Year."
36. S.D. Wells, "Over a Million People DIE from Chemotherapy Every Year, but Only 750,000 Pass Away from Cancer—What's WRONG with This Picture?," Natural News, October 25, 2019. www.natural news.com.
37. Wells, "Over a Million People DIE from Chemotherapy Every Year, but Only 750,000 Pass Away from Cancer—What's WRONG with This Picture?"
38. Quoted in Ben Child, "Cheech and Chong Star Claims Cannabis Helped Cure Prostate Cancer," *The Guardian* (Manchester, UK), May 13, 2013. www.theguardian.com.
39. Quoted in Bill Keller, "The Case Against Cannabis," Marshall Project, January 7, 2019. www.themarshallproject.org.
40. Quoted in Aisha Dow, "She Was a Nurse. So Why Did Helen Shun Conventional Cancer Treatment?," *The Age* (Melbourne, Australia), May 21, 2018. www.theage.com.au.
41. Quoted in Black Salve Alliance, "Recommendations and Reviews," Facebook, April 29, 2020. www.facebook.com.
42. Quoted in Black Salve Alliance, "Recommendations and Reviews."
43. Complementary Cancer Charity, "Black Salve—a Powerful Alternative Cancer Treatment?," September 21, 2017. www.cancerac tive.com.
44. Quoted in Rachael Rettner, "Nearly Half of Americans Think Alternative Medicine Can Cure Cancer. It Can't." Live Science, October 30, 2018. www.livescience.com.
45. Quoted in Brandy Zadrozny and Aliza Nadi, "How Anti-Vaxxers Target Grieving Moms and Turn Them into Crusaders Against Vaccines," NBC News, September 24, 2019. www.nbcnews.com.

Chapter Four: Combating Social Media Falsehoods

46. Quoted in James Temperton, "How the 5G Coronavirus Conspiracy Theory Tore Through the Internet," *Wired*, April 6, 2020. www .wired.co.uk.

47. Quoted in Temperton, "How the 5G Coronavirus Conspiracy Theory Tore Through the Internet."

48. Quoted in Ryan Gallagher, "5G Virus Conspiracy Theory Fueled by Coordinated Effort," Bloomberg, April 9, 2020. www.bloomberg.com.

49. Quoted in Gallagher, "5G Virus Conspiracy Theory Fueled by Coordinated Effort."

50. Quoted in Shona Ghosh, "Facebook Blocked 5G Conspiracy Groups with Thousands of Members After Users Celebrated the Destruction of Phone Masts," Business Insider, April 14, 2020. www.businessinsider.com.

51. Twitter Safety (@Twitter Safety), "We have broadened our guidance on unverified claims that incite people to engage in harmful activity," Twitter, April 22, 2020. https://twitter.com/TwitterSafety/status/1253044659175034880.

52. Twitter Safety (@Twitter Safety), "Since introducing our updated policies on March 18, we've removed over 2,230 Tweets containing misleading and potentially harmful content," Twitter, April 22, 2020. https://twitter.com/TwitterSafety/status/1253044734416711680.

53. Quoted in Audrey McNamara, "Facebook Announces Plan to Combat Anti-vaccine Misinformation," Daily Beast, March 7, 2019. www.thedailybeast.com.

54. Quoted in Elizabeth Cohen and John Bonifield, "Facebook to Get Tougher on Anti-vaxers," CNN, February 26, 2019. www.cnn.com.

55. Quoted in Anderson and Rainie, "The Future of Truth and Misinformation Online."

56. Quoted in Anderson and Rainie, "The Future of Truth and Misinformation Online."

57. Quoted in Anderson and Rainie, "The Future of Truth and Misinformation Online."

58. Quoted in Anderson and Rainie, "The Future of Truth and Misinformation Online."

59. Quoted in Justia, *Whitney v. California*, 274 U.S. 357 (1927). https://supreme.justia.com.

60. John Frohnmayer, *Out of Tune: Listening to the First Amendment.* Golden, CO: Fulcrum, 1995, p. 15.

61. Quoted in Eliza Relman, "Facebook Is Removing Promotions for Anti-quarantine Protests That Violate Stay-Home Orders in California, New Jersey, and Nebraska," Business Insider, April 20, 2020. www.businessinsider.com.

62. Quoted in Anderson and Rainie, "The Future of Truth and Misinformation Online."

63. Quoted in Anderson and Rainie, "The Future of Truth and Misinformation Online."

BBB Scam Tracker—www.bbb.org/scamtracker

Founded in 1912, the Better Business Bureau is a nonprofit organization whose self-described mission is to focus on advancing marketplace trust. Its BBB Scam Tracker website page provides a real-time map and a list of recently reported scams.

Common Sense Media

www.commonsensemedia.org

Common Sense Media is an independent nonprofit organization that provides education, ratings, and tools to families to promote safe technology and media for children and teens. Its goal is to help kids thrive in a world of media and technology.

FactCheck.org—www.factcheck.org

FactCheck.org is a nonprofit website with the self-described mission of reducing the level of deception and confusion in US politics. The website features a Viral Spiral section devoted to debunking social media misinformation.

Get Net Wise—www.getnetwise.org

Get Net Wise is a website supported by internet industry corporations and public interest organizations. Its goal is to ensure that internet users have safe and constructive online experiences. The website contains information about digital citizenship, media literacy, and online misinformation.

Internet & American Life Project—http://pewinternet.org

Through its Internet & American Life Project, the Pew Research Center studies how Americans use the internet and how digital technologies are shaping the world today. Its website has the results of numerous studies about social media and the internet.

Snopes—www.snopes.com

Founded in 1994, Snopes is the oldest and largest fact-checking website. Its easily searchable database allows users to see what the Snopes investigators have learned about various social media posts and other online stories. Its fact-check articles often include links to documenting sources so readers can do independent research and make up their own minds.

Books

Kathryn Hulick, *Thinking Critically: Fake News*. San Diego: ReferencePoint, 2020.

Carla Mooney, *Fake News and the Manipulation of Public Opinion*. San Diego: ReferencePoint, 2019.

Cailin O'Connor and James Owen Weatherall, *The Misinformation Age: How False Beliefs Spread*. New Haven, CT: Yale University Press, 2020.

Thomas Rid, *Active Measures: The Secret History of Disinformation and Political Warfare*. New York: Farrar, Straus and Giroux, 2020.

Kathryn Roberts, ed., *Internet Journalism and Fake News*. New York: Greenhaven, 2018.

Internet Sources

Janna Anderson and Lee Rainie, "The Future of Truth and Misinformation Online," Pew Research Center, October 19, 2017. www.pewinternet.org.

Janna Anderson and Lee Rainie, "Stories from Experts About the Impact of Digital Life," Pew Research Center, July 3, 2018. www.pewinternet.org.

Elizabeth Cohen and John Bonifield, "Facebook to Get Tougher on Anti-vaxers," CNN, February 26, 2019. www.cnn.com.

Ryan Gallagher, "5G Virus Conspiracy Theory Fueled by Coordinated Effort," Bloomberg, April 9, 2020. www.bloomberg.com.

Institute of Humane Studies, "Social Media, Tribalism, and the Prevalence of Fake News," *Big Think* (blog), June 12, 2019. https://theihs.org.

James Temperton, "How the 5G Coronavirus Conspiracy Theory Tore Through the Internet," *Wired*, April 6, 2020. www.wired.co.uk.

Brandy Zadrozny, "Social Media Hosted a Lot of Fake Health News This Year. Here's What Went Most Viral," NBC News, December 29, 2019. www.nbcnews.com.

Index